# Quotes for Nasty Women

# Quotes for Nasty Women

**EMPOWERING WISDOM from Women Who Break the Rules**

# Nasty Women

edited by Linda Picone

STERLING
New York

STERLING
New York

An Imprint of Sterling Publishing Co., Inc.
1166 Avenue of the Americas
New York, NY 10036

ISBN 978-1-4549-2782-2

Distributed in Canada by Sterling Publishing Co., Inc.
$^c$/o Canadian Manda Group, 664 Annette Street
Toronto, Ontario, Canada M6S 2C8
Distributed in the United Kingdom by GMC Distribution Services
Castle Place, 166 High Street, Lewes, East Sussex, England BN7 1XU
Distributed in Australia by NewSouth Books
45 Beach Street, Coogee, NSW 2034, Australia

For information about custom editions, special sales, and premium
and corporate purchases, please contact Sterling Special Sales
at 800-805-5489 or specialsales@sterlingpublishing.com.

Manufactured in Canada

2  4  6  8  10  9  7  5  3

sterlingpublishing.com

Book design by Christine Heun

# INTRODUCTION

There have always been strong women: women who stood up for themselves and their ideals, despite the odds; women who took on roles that weren't "ladylike"; women who refused to limit their words or their actions to what was deemed proper.

The first such woman in Judeo-Christian tradition may well have been Eve, who wasn't content to idle in the Garden of Eden but let curiosity get the better of her—and urged Adam to bite that apple as well.

The reaction to strong, sometimes outspoken, sometimes loud, sometimes downright annoying women has been both admiration, by some, and criticism, by others.

When Donald Trump referred to Hillary Clinton as "such a nasty woman" during the last presidential debate in 2016, it felt familiar to many women, no matter their politics or their feelings about Clinton. They recognized that kind of criticism, that labeling, of women who dared to stand up for themselves. Too many had experienced it in their own lives, in school, at work, even in what should have been the safety of their own homes.

Hillary Clinton had done nothing more—and nothing less—than any of the many male candidates who preceded her in presidential debates and on the campaign trail. She'd argued, made strong statements, and sometimes equivocated instead of answering a question. In short, she was a politician. But while similar behavior by male candidates is taken for granted, she was "such a nasty woman."

Although Hillary Clinton did not lay claim to the title "Nasty Woman," many others have—happily. You can find a T-shirt or a mug, an embroidered pillow or a hat. The label has become a source of pride for many women of all ages and in all walks of life.

Some Nasty Women are quiet, some are loud. Some work behind the scenes, some stand in front of crowds. Some seek out the role, some are thrust into it by circumstances. They vary greatly in historic era, philosophy, voice, and the causes they fight for—or against.

This collection of quotations by, for, and about Nasty Women includes a few women from centuries past, many from the nineteenth and twentieth centuries, and a wide range of contemporary women. Their voices are different, just as their concerns often are, but their comments and advice are consistent across generations, geography, race, and history in encouraging other women to:

>> Be yourself. If you're smart or strong or talented, use what you've got.

>> Stand up for what you believe in. For some Nasty Women, this has meant giving their lives. For many, it meant losing a comfortable place in society.

>> Don't worry about what other people think. From Joan of Arc to Mae West to Lady Gaga, Nasty Women have stood out from the crowd because they don't really care what the crowd thinks of them.

Individual Nasty Women have been silenced, at times permanently. But there always have been Nasty Women, and it's likely that there always will be.

In February 2017, U.S. Senator Elizabeth Warren made her view of the attorney general nominee Senator Jeff Sessions known. They weren't positive views. Senate Majority Leader Mitch McConnell found her in violation of a Senate rule that forbids criticizing another senator in that way. Warren continued and McConnell barred her from speaking until the hearings on the attorney general were completed.

"Sen. Warren was giving a lengthy speech," said McConnell. "She had appeared to violate the rule. She was warned. She was given an explanation.

"Nevertheless, she persisted."

As did so many Nasty Women before her.

You ought to be out raising hell. This is the fighting age. Put on your fighting clothes.

*—Mother Jones*

❋

Living is a form of not being sure, not knowing what next or how. The moment you know how, you begin to die a little.

*—Agnes de Mille*

Every word a woman writes changes the story of the world, revises the official version.

—*Carolyn See*

I thank you trolls so much. It fills me with hope and power to see you all furiously posting, so as always accuse me of whatever lies you want. Call me a whale. Call me a thief, and I will continue to rise and fight and lead.

—*Amy Schumer*

I don't want
*happy-face*
conclusions.
I want the
TRUTH.

—*Elizabeth Warren*

Avoiding danger is no safer in the long run than outright exposure. The fearful are caught as often as the bold.

—*Helen Keller*

➤➤ • ◄◄

I was the conductor of the Underground Railroad for eight years, and I can say what most conductors can't say—I never ran my train off the track, and I never lost a passenger.

—*Harriet Tubman*

What matters in a character is not whether one holds this or that opinion: what matters is how proudly one upholds it.

—*Germaine de Staël*

➤➤ • ◄◄

I like to help women help themselves, as that is, in my opinion, the best way to settle the woman question. Whatever we can do and do well, we have a right to, and I don't think anyone will deny us.

—*Louisa May Alcott*

A little stress
*and adventure*
is good for you,
if nothing else,
just to prove
YOU ARE ALIVE.

*—Lady Bird Johnson*

I don't look at what I've lost. I look instead at what I have left.

*—Betty Ford*

※

People thought I was ruthless, which I was. I didn't give a darn who was on the other side of the net. I'd knock you down if you got in my way.

*—Althea Gibson*

When a woman becomes her own best friend, life is easier.

—*Diane von Fürstenberg*

❊

Hard work keeps the wrinkles out of the mind and spirit.

—*Helena Rubinstein*

I did what my conscience told me to do, and you can't fail if you do that.

—Anita Hill

A woman with a voice is by definition a strong woman. But the search to find that voice can be remarkably difficult.

—*Melinda Gates*

⤜ • ⤛

I have learned over the years that when one's mind is made up, this diminishes fear; knowing what must be done does away with fear.

—*Rosa Parks*

Nothing is impossible; the word itself says "I'm possible."

—Audrey Hepburn

⤜ • ⤛

Love bravely, live bravely, be courageous—there's really nothing to lose. There's no wrong you can't make right again, so be kind to yourself.

—Jewel

The most common way people give up their power is by thinking they don't have any.

*—Alice Walker*

❈

A strong woman is a woman determined to do something others are determined not to be done.

*—Marge Piercy*

# We realize the importance of our voices only when we are silenced.

—*Malala Yousafzai*

You can't always be the strongest or most talented person in the room, but you can be the most competitive.

—*Pat Summitt*

I simply ache from smiling. Why are women expected to beam all the time? It's unfair. If a man looks solemn, it's automatically assumed he's a serious person, not a miserable one.

—*Queen Elizabeth II*

Be as bold as the first man or woman to eat an oyster.

—*Shirley Chisholm*

I've never asked for special treatment along the way. And I'm never going to hide the fact that I'm a girl, ever. That's obvious, isn't it?

—*Danica Patrick*

The reward for conformity is that everyone likes you except yourself.

—*Rita Mae Brown*

※

Your job is to be you, which includes being the chief beneficiary of all things you do right, the chief victim of all you do wrong, and the one person on Earth who has to live with every choice you make. As gatekeeper to your life, you're it.

—*Carolyn Hax*

Social change
is brought
about by those
*who dare and act,*
who can think
UNCONVENTIONALLY,
and who can court
unpopularity.

—*Indira Gandhi*

If you don't have a seat at the table, you're probably on the menu.

—Elizabeth Warren

Don't be so humble; you aren't that great.

—*Golda Meir*

❊

Sometimes I feel discriminated against, but it does not make me angry. It merely astonishes me. How can anyone deny themselves the pleasure of my company? It's beyond me.

—*Zora Neale Hurston*

You can never leave footprints that last if you are always walking on tiptoe.

—*Leymah Gbowee*

➤➤ • ◄◄

I firmly believe you never should spend your time being the former anything.

—*Condoleezza Rice*

Woman must not accept; she must challenge.
She must not be told how to use her freedom; she
must find out for herself. She must not be awed
by that which has been built up around her; she
must reverence that within her which struggles for
expression.

—*Margaret Sanger*

✦ • ✦

The willingness to accept responsibility for one's
own life is the source from which self-respect
springs.

—*Joan Didion*

One of the lessons that I grew up with was to always stay true to yourself and never let what somebody else says distract you from your goals. And so when I hear about negative and false attacks, I really don't invest any energy in them, because I know who I am.

—*Michelle Obama*

Changing the world doesn't happen all at once. It isn't a big bang. It's an evolution, the sum of a billion tiny sparks. And some of those sparks will have to come from you.

—*Katie Couric*

Women with money and women in power are two uncomfortable ideas in our society.

—*Candace Bushnell*

The important thing is not what they think of me, but what I think of them.

—Queen Victoria

There are some things you learn best in *calm*, and some in STORM.

—*Willa Cather*

The eagle has no fear of adversity. We need to be like the eagle and have a fearless spirit of a conqueror.

—*Joyce Meyer*

❀

I don't have any option. I'm not going to be less gay or more pretty. I can't try to have less personality or fewer controversial opinions.

—*Rachel Maddow*

We don't develop courage by being happy every day. We develop it by surviving difficult times and challenging adversity.

—*Barbara De Angelis*

➤➤ • ◄◄

Don't live down to expectations. Go out there and do something remarkable.

—*Wendy Wasserstein*

I love to see a young girl go out and grab the world by the lapels. Life's a bitch. You've got to go out and kick ass.

—*Maya Angelou*

It is not true that life is one damn thing after another; it's one damn thing over and over.

*—Edna St. Vincent Millay*

❀

I hate to hear you talk about all women as if they were fine ladies instead of rational creatures. None of us want to be in calm waters all our lives.

*—Jane Austen*

Beautiful? It's all a question of luck. I was born with good legs. As for the rest . . . beautiful, no. Amusing, yes.

—Josephine Baker

At the end
of the day,
we can *endure*
*much more*
than we
think we can.

—*Frida Kahlo*

A common misconception about strong women is that we don't need the hand-holding, the flowers, and the nice gestures, and what I've found to be true is that it's the strong women who want it the most.

—*Nicole Curtis*

If anger were mileage, I'd be a very frequent flyer, right up there in first class.

—*Gina Barreca*

So keep fightin' for freedom and justice, beloveds,
but don't you forget to have fun doin' it. Lord, let
your laughter ring forth. Be outrageous, ridicule
the fraidy-cats, rejoice in all the oddities that
freedom can produce.

—*Molly Ivins*

→> • <←

Anything you can do in excess for the wrong
reasons is exciting to me.

—*Carrie Fisher*

My recipe for life is not being afraid of myself,
afraid of what I think or of my opinions.

*—Eartha Kitt*

⇥ • ⇤

No one can figure out your worth but you.

*—Pearl Bailey*

They say it is better to be poor and happy than rich and miserable, but how about a compromise like moderately rich and just moody?

—*Princess Diana*

We are volcanoes. When we women offer our experience as our truth, as human truth, all the maps change. There are new mountains.

—*Ursula K. Le Guin*

※

Beware of monotony; it's the mother of all the deadly sins.

—*Edith Wharton*

You must remember to never cease to act because you fear you may fail.

—*Queen Lili'uokalani*

❀

Privacy and security are those things you give up when you show the world what makes you extraordinary.

—*Margaret Cho*

We are not interested in the possibilities of defeat; they do not exist.

—*Queen Victoria*

Life is a BANQUET
and most poor suckers
are *starving to death*.

—Rosalind Russell

I have very strong feelings about how you lead your life. You always look ahead, you never look back.

—*Ann Richards*

→→ • ←←

The word's out: I'm a woman, and I'm going to have trouble backing off on that. I am what I am.

—*Elizabeth Warren*

# Don't apologize for asking for what you deserve.

—*Mika Brzezinski*

# Well-behaved women seldom make history.

—*Laurel Thatcher Ulrich*

It's because I'm a feminist that I can't stand women limiting other women's imaginations. It really makes me angry.

—A. S. Byatt

❈

Winning doesn't always mean being first. Winning means you're doing better than you've ever done before.

—Bonnie Blair

If we learn to open our hearts, anyone, including the people who drive us crazy, can be our teacher.

—*Pema Chödrön*

❀

If you weigh well the strengths of our armies, you will see that in this battle we must conquer or die. This is a woman's resolve. As for the men, they may live or be slaves.

—*Boudicca*

I will *not* be triumphed over.

—*Cleopatra*

No woman can call herself free who does not control her own body.

—*Margaret Sanger*

➤ • ◄

Many receive advice; only the wise profit from it.

—*Harper Lee*

It takes a long time to get to be a diva. I mean, you gotta work at it.

—Diana Ross

My mother taught me that when you stand in the truth
and someone tells a lie about you, don't fight it.

—*Whitney Houston*

There's humor in everything. There's gotta be humor in
everything.

—*Amy Sedaris*

You take your life in your own hands, and what happens? A terrible thing: no one to blame.

—*Erica Jong*

❅

What you need is sustained outrage . . . there's far too much unthinking respect given to authority.

—*Molly Ivins*

# Being a woman has only bothered me in climbing trees.

—Frances Perkins

There are always a few *who stand up* in times of communal madness and have the courage to say that

WHAT UNITES US
IS GREATER THAN
WHAT DIVIDES US.

—*Geraldine Brooks*

People are always looking for the single magic
bullet that will totally change everything. There is
no single magic bullet.

*—Temple Grandin*

➤➤ • ◀◀

I'm going to dance in all the galaxies.

*—Elisabeth Kübler-Ross*

I want to be strong and empowered. I want to shock everybody.

—*Vanessa Hudgens*

It's not
enough to
be nice in life.
You've got to
have nerve.

—*Georgia O'Keeffe*

Nobody . . . took me seriously. They wondered why in the world I wanted to be a chemist when no women were doing that. The world was not waiting for me.

—*Gertrude B. Elion*

❀

The best piece of advice that I remember probably on a daily basis is to accept everything about me that is different. That is what makes me special.

—*Misty Copeland*

I will feel *equality has arrived* when we can elect to office women who are as INCOMPETENT AS SOME OF THE MEN who are already there.

—*Maureen Reagan*

There's no day that is the same as the day before.
So you have to be energized; you have to be
focused.

—*Hillary Clinton*

→→ • ←←

I see no reason to keep silent about my enjoyment
of the sound of my own voice as I work.

—*Muriel Spark*

A really strong woman accepts the war she went through and is ennobled by her scars.

—*Carly Simon*

➤ • ◄

The world needs strong women. There are a lot of strong women you do not see who are guiding, helping, mothering strong men. They want to remain unseen. It's kind of nice to be able to play a strong woman who is seen.

—*Ginger Rogers*

I am a strong woman with or without this other person, with or without this job, and with or without these tight pants.

—*Queen Latifah*

□

There is no sin punished more implacably by nature than the sin of resistance to change.

—*Anne Morrow Lindbergh*

I don't like girls pretending to be stupid because it's easier.

—Amy Winehouse

*Courage*, sacrifice, determination, commitment, *toughness*, heart, talent, *guts*. That's what little girls are made of; the heck with sugar and spice.

—*Bethany Hamilton*

You gain strength, courage, and confidence by every experience in which you really stop to look fear in the face. You are able to say to yourself, "I lived through this horror. I can take the next thing that comes along."

—*Eleanor Roosevelt*

❀

Remember our heritage is our power; we can know ourselves and our capacities by seeing that other women have been strong.

—*Judy Chicago*

You will do foolish things, but do them with enthusiasm.

—*Colette*

❋

Mile by mile, it's a trial; yard by yard, it's hard; but inch by inch, it's a cinch.

—*Gabrielle Giffords*

Life shrinks or expands in proportion to one's courage.

—*Anaïs Nin*

❀

Though the sex to which I belong is considered weak, you will nevertheless find me a rock that bends to no wind.

—*Queen Elizabeth I*

# First fight.

# Then fiddle.

—*Gwendolyn Brooks*

I always wondered why somebody doesn't do something about that. Then I realized I was somebody.

—Lily Tomlin

I have stood on a mountain of no's for one yes.

*—B. Smith*

✈ • ✈

Everyone shines, given the right lighting.

*—Susan Cain*

When you embrace your difference, your DNA, your look or heritage or religion or your unusual name, that's when you start to shine.

—*Bethenny Frankel*

The moment anyone tries to demean or degrade you in any way, you have to know how great you are. Nobody would bother to beat you down if you were not a threat.

—*Cicely Tyson*

I am where I am
because *I believe*
in all possibilities.

—*Whoopi Goldberg*

Don't compromise yourself. You are all you've got. There is no yesterday, no tomorrow; it's all the same day.

—*Janis Joplin*

You have to be taught to be second class; you're not born that way.

—*Lena Horne*

※

At the end of the day, it's not about equal rights, it's about how we think. We have to reshape our own perception of how we view ourselves.

—*Beyoncé*

I have come to realize making yourself happy is most important. Never be ashamed of how you feel. You have the right to feel any emotion you want and do what makes you happy. That's my life motto.

—*Demi Lovato*

You grow up the day you have your first real laugh at yourself.

—*Ethel Barrymore*

Women have a special corner of their hearts for sins they have never committed.

—*Cornelia Otis Skinner*

Without an open-minded mind, you can never be a great success.

—*Martha Stewart*

# My goal is to be accused of being strident.

—Susan Faludi

I never said I wanted a "happy" life but an interesting one. From separation and loss, I have learned a lot. I have become strong and resilient, as is the case of almost every human being exposed to life and the world. We don't even know how strong we are until we are forced to bring that hidden strength forward.

—*Isabel Allende*

❋

I want to be around a really long time. I want to be a thorn in the side of everything as long as possible.

—*Patti Smith*

There are lessons in everything. The bad, the good. Our job is to listen, and to continue to learn, so that maybe we get better at this. Maybe get better at life.

*—Laverne Cox*

➤➤ • ◄◄

You don't make progress by standing on the sidelines, whimpering and complaining. You make progress by implementing ideas.

*—Shirley Chisholm*

I'm scared all the time. You have to have fear in order to have courage. I'm a courageous person because I'm a scared person.

—*Ronda Rousey*

→→ • ←←

There's no reason that young girls shouldn't feel like they can't smash people on the field. Nothing dirty. You want to keep it clean. You just want to play hard. Get your jersey dirty, shorts dirty, and just have fun out there.

—*Carli Lloyd*

It is there to be done, so I do it.

—*Frances Perkins*

❀

You can waste your life drawing lines. Or you can
live your life crossing them.

—*Shonda Rhimes*

If someone calls
you *bossy* because
YOU DIDN'T LET
THEM PUSH YOU
around, so be it.

—*Mary Barra*

I think that if you shake the tree, you ought to be around when the fruit falls to pick it up.

—*Mary Cassatt*

I have made my world and it is a much better world than I ever saw outside.

—*Louise Nevelson*

❏

We ask ourselves, "Who am I to be brilliant, gorgeous, talented, fabulous?" Actually, who are you not to be?

—*Marianne Williamson*

I get angry about things, then go on and work.

—Toni Morrison

The ultimate goal is to be an interesting, useful, wholesome person. If you're successful on top of that, then you're way ahead of everybody.

—*Martha Stewart*

❀

You have to make mistakes to find out who you aren't. You take the action, and the insight follows: You don't think your way into becoming yourself.

—*Anne Lamott*

A person without curiosity may as well be dead.

—Judy Blume

→> • <←

I don't really want to become normal, average,
standard. I want merely to gain in strength, in the
courage to live out my life more fully, enjoy more,
experience more. I want to develop even more
original and more unconventional traits.

—Anaïs Nin

If you obey
all the rules,
you miss all
the fun.

—Katharine Hepburn

You shall *know the truth*, and the truth will MAKE YOU ODD.

—*Flannery O'Connor*

No person is your friend who demands your silence, or denies your right to grow.

—*Alice Walker*

I've gone from saint to whore and back to saint again, all in one lifetime.

—*Ingrid Bergman*

# Always be a first-rate version of yourself instead of a second-rate version of somebody else.

—*Judy Garland*

All of my life I have always had the urge to do things better than anybody else.

—*Babe Didrikson Zaharias*

A lot of people are afraid to say what they want.
That's why they don't get what they want.

—*Madonna*

❀

Courage is like a muscle. We strengthen it by use.

—*Ruth Gordon*

My theory is, strong people don't need strong leaders.

*—Ella Baker*

❀

It's kind of rebellious to be yourself.

*—Kate Moss*

What's really terrible is to pretend that the second-rate is the first-rate. To pretend that you don't need love when you do, or you like your work when you know quite well you're capable of better.

—*Doris Lessing*

You just do it. You force yourself to get up. You force yourself to put one foot before the other and, God damn it, you refuse to let it get to you. You fight. You cry. You curse. Then you go about the business of living. That's how I've done it. There's no other way.

—*Elizabeth Taylor*

# Darling, the legs aren't so beautiful, I just know what to do with them.

—*Marlene Dietrich*

Women should try to *increase their size* rather than decrease it, because I believe the bigger we are, the more space we'll take up, and the MORE WE'LL HAVE TO BE RECKONED WITH.

—*Roseanne Barr*

My legacy is that I stayed on course . . . from
the beginning to the end, because I believed in
something inside of me.

—*Tina Turner*

➤➤ • ◄◄

To succeed in life, you need three things: a
wishbone, a backbone, and a funny bone.

—*Reba McEntire*

My only ambition is to be true every moment I am living.

—*Juliette Binoche*

❃

You can't control how other people see you or think of you. But you have to be comfortable with that.

—*Helen Mirren*

I'm crazy
and I don't
pretend to be
anything else.

—*Rihanna*

# I'm an architect, not just a woman architect.

—*Zaha Hadid*

# I don't think there are any rude questions.

—Helen Thomas

You can't move mountains by whispering at them.

*—Pink*

➤ • ◀

I feel myself becoming the fearless person I have dreamt of being. Have I arrived? No. But I'm constantly evolving and challenging myself to be unafraid to make mistakes.

*—Janelle Monáe*

➤ • ◀

Cautious, careful people always casting about to preserve their reputations can never effect a reform.

*—Susan B. Anthony*

I urge you to
be as impudent
as you dare.
BE BOLD,
BE BOLD,
BE BOLD.

—*Susan Sontag*

Becoming yourself is really hard and confusing, and it's a process. It's often not cool to be the person who puts themselves out there.

—*Emma Watson*

I never thought of myself as being in the avant-garde. I said what I had to say, as I was able to say it.

—*Simone de Beauvoir*

If you're creating anything at all, it's really dangerous to care about what people think.

—*Kristen Wiig*

I am interested in telling my particular truth as I have seen it.

—*Gwendolyn Brooks*

I hated conventional art. I began to live.

—*Mary Cassatt*

A woman who is willing to be herself and pursue her own potential runs not so much the risk of loneliness as the challenge of exposure to more interesting men—and people in general.

—*Lorraine Hansberry*

# Your thorns are the best part of you.

—Marianne Moore

To fly, we have to have resistance.

*—Maya Lin*

❀

We're all strange inside. We learn how to disguise our differences as we grow up.

*—Annie Proulx*

❀

When things are really dismal, you can laugh, or you can cave in completely.

*—Margaret Atwood*

There are chapters in every life which are seldom read and certainly not aloud.

—*Carol Shields*

❀

I ain't afraid to love a man. I ain't afraid to shoot him, either.

—*Annie Oakley*

# Never let go of that fiery sadness called desire.

—*Patti Smith*

The success of every woman should be the inspiration to another. We should raise each other up. Make sure you're very courageous: Be strong, be extremely kind, and above all be humble.

*—Serena Williams*

I trust my instincts. I don't distrust them. They haven't led me astray. It's when I've made up my mind to be efficient that is when I have gone wrong.

*—Dorothea Lange*

You've got to have something to eat and a little love in your life before you can hold still for any damn body's sermon on how to behave.

*—Billie Holiday*

My life has been wonderful. I have done what I felt like. I was given courage and I was given adventure and that has carried me along. And then also a sense of humor and a little bit of common sense. It has been a very rich life.

—*Ingrid Bergman*

→→ • ←←

I say if I'm beautiful. I say if I'm strong. You will not determine my story—I will.

—*Amy Schumer*

Some women choose to follow men, and some women choose to follow their dreams. If you're wondering which way to go, remember that your career will never wake up and tell you that it doesn't love you anymore.

*—Lady Gaga*

❊

People will say to me, "You've played so many strong women" and I'll say, "Have you ever said to a man, 'You've played so many strong men'?" No! The expectation is [men] are varied. Why can't we have that expectation about women?

*—Meryl Streep*

My passions were all gathered together like fingers that made a fist. Drive is considered aggression today; I knew it then as purpose.

—*Bette Davis*

You will never truly know yourself, or the strength of your relationships, until both have been tested by adversity.

—*J. K. Rowling*

Difficult times have helped me to understand better than before how infinitely rich and beautiful life is in every way, and that so many things that one goes worrying about are of no importance whatsoever.

—*Isak Dinesen*

Show me a person who doesn't like to laugh and I'll show you a person with a toe tag.

—*Julia Roberts*

I used to be an optimist, but now I know that nothing is going to turn out as I expect.

—*Sandra Bullock*

Considering how dangerous everything is, nothing is really very frightening.

—*Gertrude Stein*

I dwell in possibility.

—*Emily Dickinson*

When anger
spreads through
the breath, guard
thy tongue from
barking idly.

—Sappho

There is a great deal of unmapped country within us, which would have to be taken into account in an explanation of our gusts and storms.

—George Eliot

❈

Trust your instincts . . . good relationships feel good. They feel right. They don't hurt. They're not painful.

—Michelle Obama

I will not have my life narrowed down. I will not bow down to somebody else's whim or to someone else's ignorance.

—*bell hooks*

→→ • ←←

[To William Butler Yeats:] Poets should never marry. The world should thank me for not marrying you.

—*Maud Gonne*

*Reputation* is what others think about you. What's far more important is *character*, because that is what you think about yourself.

—*Billie Jean King*

# Do your thing and don't care if they like it.

—*Tina Fey*

Because I am a woman, I must make unusual efforts to succeed. If I fail, no one will say, "She doesn't have what it takes." They will say, "Women don't have what it takes."

—*Clare Boothe Luce*

✳

One of the things being in politics has taught me is that men are not a reasoned or reasonable sex.

—*Margaret Thatcher*

Once you figure out what respect tastes like, it tastes better than attention. But you have to get there.

—*Pink*

I do know one thing about me: I don't measure myself by others' expectations or let others define my worth.

—*Sonia Sotomayor*

Oh, if I could but live another century and see the fruition of all the work for women! There is so much yet to be done.

*—Susan B. Anthony*

→> • <←

I wish people wouldn't think of me as a saint—unless they agree with the definition of a saint that a saint's a sinner who goes on trying.

*—Aung San Suu Kyi*

→> • <←

When we are struck at without reason, we should strike back again very hard; I am sure we should—so hard as to teach the person who struck at us never to do it again.

*—Charlotte Brontë*

You may impose *silence* upon me, but you can not prevent me from *thinking*.

—*George Sand*

The size of your dreams must always exceed your current capacity to achieve them. If your dreams do not scare you, they are not big enough.

—*Ellen Johnson Sirleaf*

❄

Toughness doesn't have to come in a pinstripe suit.

—*Dianne Feinstein*

❄

For someone with such an intense need to be liked, you'd think I would have figured out a way to be less of an asshole.

—*Anna Kendrick*

I know what I want, and I know what needs to be done to make my performance better. So I do these little askings, about the lights and costumes. It's not the diva speaking. It's the artist who knows how it has to be done.

—*Anna Netrebko*

If you want to live your life through to the end, you have to live dangerously.

—*Jeanne Moreau*

I am shocking, impertinent, and insolent. That's how it is.

—*Brigitte Bardot*

Always be more than you appear and never appear to be more than you are.

—Angela Merkel

It's your outlook on life that counts. If you take yourself lightly and don't take yourself too seriously, pretty soon you can *find the humor* in our everyday lives. And sometimes it can be a lifesaver.

—*Betty White*

If there is a job that you feel passionate about,
do what you can to pursue that job; if there is a
purpose about which you are passionate, dedicate
yourself to that purpose.

*—Janet Yellen*

→→ • ←←

It's the good girls who keep the diaries; the bad
girls never have the time.

*—Tallulah Bankhead*

→→ • ←←

I never will have peace of mind. I'm not
constructed that way. Some things in life can be
horrible.

*—Julie Christie*

Follow your instincts and do not let other people's opinion of you become your opinion of yourself.

—*Sarah Jessica Parker*

❀

In societies where men are truly confident of their own worth, women are not merely tolerated but valued.

—*Aung San Suu Kyi*

❀

And we also know that when a woman stands up and speaks truth to power, that there will be attempts to put her down, and so I'm not going to be put down. I'm not going to go anywhere.

—*Maxine Waters*

I was smart enough to go through any door that opened.

—*Joan Rivers*

The inference is that the men alone render useful service. But neither man nor woman eats these things until the woman has prepared it. The theory that the man who raises corn does a more important piece of work than the woman who makes it into bread is absurd.

—*Ida M. Tarbell*

That brain of mine is something more than merely mortal, as time will show.

—*Ada Lovelace*

Any time women come together with a collective intention, it's a powerful thing. Whether it's sitting down making a quilt, in a kitchen preparing a meal, in a club reading the same book, or around the table playing cards, or planning a birthday party, when women come together with a collective intention, magic happens.

—*Phylicia Rashad*

There are women who make things better, there are women who change things, there are women who make things happen, who make a difference. I want to be one of those women.

—*Vera Farmiga*

I think sometimes women who are supposed to be strong are also written as mean and vindictive.

—*Yancy Butler*

I only want people around me who can do the impossible.

—*Elizabeth Arden*

You have
to be willing
to offend
to make
progress.

—Claire McCaskill

A surplus of
effort could
overcome
a deficit of
confidence.

—Sonia Sotomayor

I was always willing to take a great deal of
the burden of getting along in life on my own
shoulders, but I wasn't willing to give myself a pat
on the back. I was always looking to somebody else
to give me that. That was all wrong.

*—Raquel Welch*

→→ • ←←

Life is about not knowing, having to change,
taking the moment and making the best of it,
without knowing what's going to happen next.

*—Gilda Radner*

Each time we don't say what we wanna say, we're dying.

—*Yoko Ono*

—➤ • ◄—

It is not the question, what am I going to be when I grow up; you should ask the question, who am I going to be when I grow up.

—*Goldie Hawn*

—➤ • ◄—

At a very young age, I decided I was not going to follow women's rules.

—*Joan Jett*

It's one thing to live my own life and know that I'm okay. But there's another thing I want to take on, and that is letting people know that they're okay, too.

—*Samira Wiley*

�֎

When I was younger, I was kind of fearless. I think it takes more courage to do things when you know more. I was completely naïve and I was like, "Why can't I do anything I want to do?"

—*Carole King*

✷

What's the worst that can happen? If it doesn't do well, I can put on my big girl panties, deal with it, and move on.

—*Halle Berry*

I have bursts
of being a lady,
but it doesn't
last long.

—*Shelley Winters*

I was raised to sense what someone wanted me to be and be that kind of person. It took me a long time not to judge myself through someone else's eyes.

—*Sally Field*

□

I've never backed down from a fight and I relish a good debate.

—*Olympia Snowe*

□

No one is going to feel sorry for you, so you have to go out there and be fierce.

—*Gabby Douglas*

Don't look
at your feet to
see if you are
doing it right.
JUST DANCE.

—*Anne Lamott*

What is sad for women of my generation is that they weren't supposed to work if they had families. What were they going to do when the children are grown—watch the raindrops coming down the window pane?

—*Jackie Kennedy*

I am often drawn to what appear at first to be "dark" or "difficult" subjects, but which, upon further examination, are always and only reflections of the ways human beings attempt, however clumsily, badly, or well, to connect with others.

—*Marya Hornbacher*

→ • ←

I have never tried to copy a man. I think it's very important that a woman remembers that she is a woman and not a man. You're a woman, so keep being a woman and show women and men that you are a woman. This sends the very important message that women are equal to men.

—*Vigdís Finnbogadóttir*

Do your best, one shot at a time, and then move on.

—*Nancy Lopez*

➤ • ◄

A woman's ability to make everyone in the room feel at home . . . should never be construed as weakness.

—*Benazir Bhutto*

➤ • ◄

There's a big, wonderful world out there for you. It belongs to you. It's exciting and stimulating and rewarding. Don't cheat yourselves out of this promise.

—*Nancy Reagan*

The question
isn't who's going
to *let me*;
it's
who's going
to STOP ME.

—*Ayn Rand*

Who am I? I'm my husband's wife and I'm striving to be my own person.

—*Marian Javits*

❀

Always go with the choice that scares you the most, because that's the one that is going to require the most from you.

—*Caroline Myss*

❀

Normal is not something to aspire to, it's something to get away from.

—*Jodie Foster*

That's what being young is all about. You have the courage and the daring to think that you can make a difference. You're not prone to measure your energies in time. You're not likely to live by equations.

—*Ruby Dee*

❊

I'm a multifaceted woman and person, like all women are—there's no black and white. We have shades of grey in the middle. And even many more colors that other people don't see.

—*Shakira*

Smiling doesn't win you gold medals.

—*Simone Biles*

My advice to women in general: Even if you're doing a nine-to-five job, treat yourself like a boss. Not arrogant, but be sure of what you want—and don't allow people to run anything for you without your knowledge.

—*Nicki Minaj*

I'm one of those women who's not to be messed with. I'm very opinionated and boisterous at times. I'm also kind and humble. I know when to fold and when to hold, and that's important. If my edge scares you, then you have a choice to remove yourself.

—*LisaRaye McCoy*

You are unique, and if that is not fulfilled, then something has been lost.

*—Martha Graham*

You can't be that kid standing at the top of the waterslide, overthinking it. You have to go down the chute.

*—Tina Fey*

Smart women love smart men more than smart men love smart women.

*—Natalie Portman*

# Stop wearing your wishbone where your backbone ought to be.

—*Elizabeth Gilbert*

Women are so strong and knowledgeable. You know, instead of competing with each other, I would love to complete each other. Take away that wall of competition and say, "Hey, let's just all get together and help each other be brilliant."

—*Marie Osmond*

→→ • ←←

I have a mouth and I'm not afraid to use it.

—*Megan Fox*

In silence—and in self-defense—I figured things out in my own little way.

*—Loretta Young*

❀

When you come to a roadblock, take a detour.

*—Barbara Bush*

❀

The more our societies empower women, the more we receive in return.

*—Queen Rania of Jordan*

Take chances, make mistakes. That's how you grow. Pain nourishes your courage. You have to fail in order to practice being brave.

—*Mary Tyler Moore*

If you believe in your heart that you are right, you must *fight with all your might* to do it your way. Only dead fish swim with the stream all the time.

—*Linda Ellerbee*

I think of life itself now as a wonderful play that I've written for myself, and so my purpose is to HAVE THE UTMOST FUN PLAYING MY PART.

—*Shirley MacLaine*

Most of us have trouble juggling. The woman who says she doesn't is someone whom I admire but have never met.

—*Barbara Walters*

❄

The reason why women effect so little and are so shallow is because their aims are low—marriage is the prize for which they strive; if foiled in that they rarely rise above disappointment.

—*Sarah Moore Grimké*

There has never been and never again will be a human being like you. There is nothing ordinary about you. If you feel ordinary, it is because you have chosen to hide the extraordinary parts of yourself from the world.

—*Barbara De Angelis*

❀

Humor is the shock absorber of life; it helps us take the blows.

—*Peggy Noonan*

I cannot and will not cut my conscience to fit this year's fashions.

—Lillian Hellman

Life is always a tightrope or a feather bed. Give me the tightrope.

—*Edith Wharton*

➤➤ • ◄◄

This journey has always been about reaching your own other shore, no matter what it is, and that dream continues.

—*Diana Nyad*

➤➤ • ◄◄

Do the one thing you think you cannot do. Fail at it. Try again. Do better the second time. The only people who never tumble are those who never mount the high wire. This is your moment. Own it.

—*Oprah Winfrey*

Slow down? Rest? With all eternity before me?

—*Sarah Bernhardt*

Take your work seriously, but never yourself.

—*Dame Margot Fonteyn*

I sing to the realists, people who accept it like it is.

—*Aretha Franklin*

If I'm *too strong* for some people, THAT'S THEIR PROBLEM.

—*Glenda Jackson*

When I dare to be powerful, to use my strength in the service of my vision, then it becomes less and less important whether I am afraid.

—*Audre Lorde*

That disturbs people when they know they didn't
have the guts or integrity to stick to their dreams.

—*Sandra Bernhard*

❀

I always wanted to be normal. I tried really hard,
but it's like I try so hard and then people still say
I'm offbeat. I've learned to accept that and take
advantage of it as an actor.

—*Zooey Deschanel*

❀

You don't have to like everybody, but you have to
love everybody.

—*Fannie Lou Hamer*

# Put yourself in the

path of lightning.

—*Valerie Jarrett*

Patience is a virtue, but impatience gets things done.

—Chelsea Clinton

❁

Of all the nasty outcomes predicted for women's liberation . . . none was more alarming . . . than the suggestion that women would eventually become just like men.

—Barbara Ehrenreich

Let the world know you as you are, not as you think you should be, because sooner or later, if you are posing, you will forget the pose and then where are you?

—*Fanny Brice*

Never underestimate the power of dreams and the influence of the human spirit. We are all the same in this notion: The potential for greatness lives within each of us.

—*Wilma Rudolph*

✦

I spent an awful lot of my life underestimating myself and, as a result, not exceeding my own expectations.

—*Jane Pauley*

✦

God made men stronger but not necessarily more intelligent. He gave women intuition and femininity. And, used properly, that combination easily jumbles the brain of any man I've ever met.

—*Farrah Fawcett*

There are many persons ready to do what is right because in their hearts they know it is right. But they hesitate, waiting for the other fellow to make the first move—and he, in turn, waits for you.

—*Marian Anderson*

➤➤ • ⬅⬅

I've never had a humble opinion. If you've got an opinion, why be humble about it?

—*Joan Baez*

The thing
women have
yet to learn is
nobody gives
you power.
You just take it.

—Roseanne Barr

Some guy said to me: "Don't you think you're too old to sing rock 'n' roll?" I said: "You better check with Mick Jagger."

—*Cher*

❀

The master class seldom lose a chance to insult a woman who has the ability for something besides service to his lordship.

—*Caroline Nichols Churchill*

Stop telling girls they can be anything they want when they grow up. . . . Because it would've never occurred to them that they couldn't.

—*Sarah Silverman*

❀

To feel valued, to know, even if only once in a while, that you can do a job well is an absolutely marvelous feeling.

—*Barbara Walters*

❀

I'd rather regret the things I've done than regret the things I haven't done.

—*Lucille Ball*

Good girls
go to heaven,
bad girls go
everywhere.

—Mae West

I really wanted to be nasty and mean and bad. It's so much easier than being the good girl.

—*Robin Tunney*

<br>

Keep your dreams alive. Understand to achieve anything requires faith and belief in yourself, vision, hard work, determination, and dedication. Remember all things are possible for those who believe.

—*Gail Devers*

If we mean to have heroes, statesmen, and philosophers, we should have learned women.

—*Abigail Adams*

■

Whatsoever it is morally right for a man to do, it is morally right for a woman to do.

—*Angelina Grimké*

I've always known I was gifted, which is not the easiest thing in the world for a person to know, because you're not responsible for your gift, only for what you do with it.

*—Hazel Scott*

❀

I naturally want to be provocative.

*—Iggy Azalea*

❀

I cannot tolerate fools—won't have anything to do with them. I only want to associate with brilliant people.

*—Ida Lupino*

I want to live my life, not record it.

—*Jackie Kennedy*

We still think of a powerful man as a born leader and a powerful woman as an anomaly.

—Margaret Atwood

My candle burns at both ends; it will not last the night; but ah, my foes, and oh, my friends—it gives a lovely light!

—*Edna St. Vincent Millay*

➤ • ◄

Lock up your libraries if you like; but there is no gate, no lock, no bolt that you can set upon the freedom of my mind.

—*Virginia Woolf*

➤ • ◄

The first thing I do in the morning is brush my teeth and sharpen my tongue.

—*Dorothy Parker*

We work on macro issues and macaroni-and-cheese issues. When women are in the halls of power, our national debate reflects the needs and dreams of American families.

*—Barbara Mikulski*

❋

Life begets life. Energy creates energy. It is by spending oneself that one becomes rich.

*—Sarah Bernhardt*

❋

I was a woman, a divorcee, a socialist, an agnostic . . . all possible sins together.

*—Michelle Bachelet*

My dreams were all my own; I accounted for them to nobody; they were my refuge when annoyed— *my dearest pleasure* when free.

—*Mary Shelley*

I've learned from experience that the greater part of our happiness or misery depends on our dispositions and not on our circumstances.

—*Martha Washington*

>> • <<

I hope the fathers and mothers of little girls will look at them and say, "Yes, women can."

—*Dilma Rousseff*

>> • <<

The art of life is not controlling what happens to us, but using what happens to us.

—*Gloria Steinem*

The worst thing that we can do as women is not stand up for each other, and this is something we can practice every day, no matter where we are and what we do—women sticking up for other women, choosing to protect and celebrate each other instead of competing or criticizing one another.

—*Amal Clooney*

To be a rebel is not to be a revolutionary. It is more often by a way of spinning one's wheels deeper in sand.

*—Kate Millett*

I do not make any apologies for my manner or personality. I come from a long line of very strong, black African-American women who neither bend nor bow. I haven't had very good modeling in submission.

*—Faye Wattleton*

Pain is real when you get other people to believe in it. If no one believes in it but you, your pain is madness or hysteria.

*—Naomi Wolf*

There are some
people who still
feel threatened
by strong women.
*That's their problem.*
IT'S NOT MINE.

—*Gloria Allred*

# Don't let them tame you.

—*Isadora Duncan*

I've always been motivated more by negative comments than by positive ones. I know what I do well. Tell me what I don't do well.

—*Abby Wambach*

※

If you rest, you rust.

—*Helen Hayes*

※

Being a lady does not require silence.

—*Betty Ford*

When I was younger there was something in me. I had passion. I may not have known what I was going to do with that passion, but there was something—and I still feel it. It's this little engine that roars inside of me and I just want to keep going and going.

—*Sheila Johnson*

Need, yearn, and work—that is the kind of aggression that brings success, not acting dramatic.

—*Helen Gurley Brown*

I began wearing hats as a young lawyer because it helped me to establish my professional identity. Before that, whenever I was at a meeting, someone would ask me to get coffee.

—*Bella Abzug*

Only she who attempts the absurd can achieve the impossible.

—*Robin Morgan*

Sometimes people try to destroy you, precisely because they recognize your power. Not because they don't see it, but because they see it and they don't want it to exist.

—*bell hooks*

We are, as a sex,
infinitely superior to
men, and if we were
free and developed,
healthy in body
and mind, as we
should be under

natural conditions, our motherhood would be our glory. That function gives women such wisdom and power as no male can possess.

—*Elizabeth Cady Stanton*

We need women who are at the head of a boardroom, like at the head of the White House, at the head of kind of major scientific enterprises so that little girls everywhere can then think, "You know what? I can do that, I want to do that, I will do that."

—*Chelsea Clinton*

❋

I am a mystery to myself.

—*Angelina Grimké*

Wolves and women are relational by nature, inquiring, possessed of great endurance and strength. They are deeply intuitive, intensely concerned with their young, their mate, and their pack. Yet both have been hounded, harassed, and falsely imputed to be devouring and devious, overly aggressive, of less value than those who are their detractors.

—*Clarissa Pinkola Estés*

❁

Of any stopping place in life, it is good to ask whether it will be a good place from which to go on as well as a good place to remain.

—*Mary Catherine Bateson*

Always remember that you are absolutely unique.
Just like everyone else.

—*Margaret Mead*

➤➤ • ◂◂

So whatever you want to do, just do it. . . . Making
a damn fool of yourself is absolutely essential. And
you will have a great time.

—*Gloria Steinem*

**Real integrity is doing the right thing, knowing that nobody's going to know whether you did it or not.**

—*Oprah Winfrey*

Women are in league with each other, a secret conspiracy of hearts and pheromones.

—Camille Paglia

I've been described as a tough and noisy woman, a prize fighter, a man-hater—you name it. They call me Battling Bella, Mother Courage, and a Jewish mother with more complaints than Portnoy.

—*Bella Abzug*

❀

I myself have never been able to find out precisely what feminism is: I only know that people call me a feminist whenever I express sentiments that differentiate me from a doormat or a prostitute.

—*Rebecca West*

Women have very little idea of how much men hate them.

—*Germaine Greer*

When you're a girl, you have to be everything. You have to be dope at what you do, but you have to be super sweet, and you have to be sexy, and you have to be this, and you have to be that, and you have to be nice. . . . I can't be all of those things at once. I'm a human being.

—*Nicki Minaj*

It is very hard to be a female leader. While it is assumed that any man, no matter how tough, has a soft side . . . any female leader is assumed to be one-dimensional.

—*Billie Jean King*

A woman is like a tea bag—you can't tell how strong she is until you put her in hot water.

—*Eleanor Roosevelt*

It was a very cool thing to be a smart girl, as opposed to some other, different kind. And I think that made a great deal of difference to me growing up and in my life afterward.

—*Elena Kagan*

Every life has its actual blanks, which the ideal must fill up, or which else remain bare and profitless forever.

—*Julia Ward Howe*

I was gravely warned by some of my female acquaintances that no woman could expect to be regarded as a lady after she had written a book.

—*Lydia Maria Child*

✳

If the first woman God ever made was strong enough to turn the world upside down all alone, these women together ought to be able to turn it back and get it right side up again.

—*Sojourner Truth*

You have to make more noise than anybody else, you have to make yourself more obtrusive than anybody else, you have to fill all the papers more than anybody else, in fact you have to be there all the time and see that they do not snow you under, if you are really going to get your reform realized.

—*Emmeline Pankhurst*

It is our duty
to make
this world a
better place
for women.

—*Christabel Pankhurst*

Women have always been an equal part of the past. We just haven't been a part of history.

—*Gloria Steinem*

Someday, somehow, I am going to do something useful, something for people. They are, most of them, so helpless, so hurt, and so unhappy.

—*Edith Cavell*

→→ • ←←

A gentleman opposed to their enfranchisement once said to me, "Women have never produced anything of any value to the world." I told him the chief product of the women had been the men, and left it to him to decide whether the product was of any value.

—*Anna Howard Shaw*

I knew well that the only way I could get that door open was to knock it down; because I knocked all of them down.

—*Sadie Tanner Mossell Alexander*

❀

Depart from discretion when it interferes with duty.

—*Hannah More*

❀

I never wanted to feel I hadn't worked hard enough.

—*Kristi Yamaguchi*

I tell you,
in this world,
being a little
crazy helps to
*keep you sane.*

—*Zsa Zsa Gabor*

This life is what you make it. No matter what, you're going to mess up sometimes, it's a universal truth.

But the good part is you get to decide how you're going to mess it up.

—Marilyn Monroe

Never limit yourself because of others' limited imagination; never limit others because of your own limited imagination.

—*Mae Jemison*

Life is not easy for any of us. But what of that? We must have perseverance and, above all, confidence in ourselves. We must believe we are gifted for something and that this thing must be attained.

—*Marie Curie*

I'm sick and tired of being sick and tired.

—Fannie Lou Hamer

# Channel your outrage. . . . Do that which you are able to do.

—Kathy Reichs

The argument between wives and whores is an old one; each one thinking that whatever she is, at least she is not the other.

—*Andrea Dworkin*

❀

Whoever said anybody has a right to give up?

—*Marian Wright Edelman*

"God's plan" is often a front for men's plans and a cover for inadequacy, ignorance, and evil.

—*Mary Daly*

➤➤ • ◄◄

I had to make my own living and my own opportunity. But I made it! Don't sit down and wait for the opportunities to come. Get up and make them.

—*Madame C. J. Walker*

Right is right, even if no one else does it.

*—Juliette Gordon Low*

→> • <←

Nine-tenths of our suffering is caused by others not thinking so much of us as we think they ought.

*—Mary Lyon*

The history of progress is written in the blood of men and women who have dared to espouse an unpopular cause, as, for instance, the black man's right to his body, or woman's right to her soul.

—*Emma Goldman*

❋

The appetite grows for what it feeds on.

—*Ida B. Wells*

I am a woman who enjoys herself very much;
sometimes I lose, sometimes I win.

—*Mata Hari*

❁

One life is all we have and we live it as we believe
in living it. But to sacrifice what you are and to live
without belief, that is a fate more terrible than dying.

—*Joan of Arc*

I refused to take no for an answer.

—*Bessie Coleman*

My experience in childhood and adolescence of the subordinate role played by the female in a society run entirely by men had convinced me that I was not cut out to be a wife.

—*Rita Levi-Montalcini*

There's something contagious about demanding freedom.

—Robin Morgan

No one
can take
advantage
of you
without your
permission.

—Ann Landers

I want to do it because I want to do it. Women must try to do things as men have tried. When they fail, their failure must be but a challenge to others.

—*Amelia Earhart*

❅

You can be the lead in your own life.

—*Kerry Washington*

The question was asked, "How can you be a mother and a congresswoman?" I said, "I have a brain, I have a uterus, and they both work."

—*Patricia Schroeder*

➤➤ • ◄◄

Anybody who's ever dealt with me knows not to mess with me.

—*Nancy Pelosi*

I make the most
of all that comes
and the least of
all that goes.

—*Sara Teasdale*

Humility is no substitute for a good personality.

—*Fran Lebowitz*

You have trust in what you think. If you splinter yourself and try to please everyone, you can't.

—*Annie Leibovitz*

You are what you are when nobody is looking.

—*Abigail Van Buren*

People ask me sometimes, "When will there be enough women on the court?" And my answer is: "When there are nine."

—Ruth Bader Ginsburg

For me, it seems to help me take the pressure off if I don't pay attention to what other people are telling me.

—*Missy Franklin*

❋

A leader takes people where they want to go
A great leader takes people where they don't necessarily want to go, but ought to be.

—*Rosalynn Carter*

Once we give up searching for approval, we often find it easier to earn respect.

—*Gloria Steinem*

We must trust our own thinking. Trust where we're going. And get the job done.

—Wilma Mankiller

I embrace the label of bad feminist because I am human. I am messy. I'm not trying to be an example. I am not trying to be perfect. I am not trying to say I have all the answers. I am not trying to say I'm right. I am just trying—trying to support what I believe in, trying to do some good in this world, trying to make some noise with my writing while also being myself.

—*Roxane Gay*

If you just set out to be liked, you would be prepared to compromise on anything at any time, and you would achieve nothing.

—*Margaret Thatcher*

I shall not change my course because those who assume to be better than I desire it.

*—Victoria Woodhull*

❀

I've been reckless, but I'm not a rebel without a cause.

*—Angelina Jolie*

❀

Success breeds confidence.

*—Beryl Markham*

If you look at what you have in life, you'll always have more. If you look at what you don't have in life, you'll never have enough.

—*Oprah Winfrey*

There are whole precincts of voters in this country whose united intelligence does not equal that of one representative American woman.

—*Carrie Chapman Catt*

It will not do
to say that it is
out of woman's
sphere to assist in
making laws, for if
that were so, then
it should be also
out of her sphere
to submit to them.

—*Amelia Bloomer*

The most difficult thing is to act; the rest is merely tenacity.

—*Amelia Earhart*

One of the secrets to staying young is to always do things you don't know how to do, to keep learning.

—*Ruth Reichl*

Be first and be lonely.

—*Ginni Rometty*

I found out along the way that they like you a little imperfect.

—*Lena Horne*

❄

You can best fight any existing evil from the inside.

—*Hattie McDaniel*

As a man gets more successful, he is better liked by men and women, and as a woman gets more successful, she is less liked by men and women.

—*Sheryl Sandberg*

Never having failed, I could not picture what failure meant.

—*Nellie Bly*

Don't call me a saint. I don't want to be dismissed that easily.

—*Dorothy Day*

Everything I do is for my people.

*—Sacagawea*

→→ • ←←

I know I can do more good by being vocal than by staying quiet. I'd have a whole lot more money if I lied, but I wouldn't enjoy spending it.

*—Martina Navratilova*

→→ • ←←

If you think taking care of yourself is selfish, change your mind. If you don't, you're simply ducking your responsibilities.

*—Ann Richards*

When you can't find someone to follow, you have to find a way to lead by example.

—Roxane Gay

There is no social-change fairy. There is only change made by the hands of individuals.

—*Winona LaDuke*

Greatness is not measured by what a man or woman accomplishes, but by the opposition he or she has overcome to reach his goals.

—*Dorothy Height*

※

This world taught woman nothing skillful and then said her work was valueless. It permitted her no opinions and said she did not know how to think. It forbade her to speak in public and said the sex had no orators.

—*Carrie Chapman Catt*

Of course I am *not worried about intimidating men*. The type of man who will be intimidated by me is exactly the type of man I have no interest in.

—*Chimamanda Ngozi Adichie*

You don't choose the times you live in, but you do choose who you want to be. And you do choose how you think.

*—Grace Lee Boggs*

You have to act as if it were possible to radically transform the world. And you have to do it all the time.

*—Angela Davis*

Idealists foolish enough to throw caution to the winds have advanced mankind and have enriched the world.

—*Emma Goldman*

❀

Doubt is a killer. You just have to know who you are and what you stand for.

—*Jennifer Lopez*

# We are the women men warned us about.

—*Robin Morgan*

I'm an old woman. I have gray hair, many wrinkles, and arthritis in both hands. And I CELEBRATE MY FREEDOM from bureaucratic restraints that once held me.

—*Maggie Kuhn*

Cherish what makes you unique, 'cause you're really a yawn if it goes.

—*Bette Midler*

I always feel the movement is a sort of mosaic. Each of us puts in one little stone and then you get a great mosaic at the end.

—*Alice Paul*

Take criticism seriously, but not personally. If there is truth or merit in the criticism, try to learn from it. Otherwise, let it roll right off you.

—Hillary Clinton

Feel empowered. And if you start to do it, if you start to feel your voice heard, you will never go back.

—*Mary Robinson*

→→ • ←←

The torment that so many young women know, bound hand and foot by love and motherhood, without having forgotten their former dreams.

—*Simone de Beauvoir*

Whenever I don't know whether to fight or not, I fight.

—*Emily Murphy*

❄

It takes a great deal of courage to stand up to your enemies, but a great deal more to stand up to your friends.

—*J. K. Rowling*

The people I'm furious with are the women's liberationists. They keep getting up on soapboxes and proclaiming women are brighter than men. That's true, but it should be kept quiet or it ruins the whole racket.

—*Anita Loos*

❃

I'm always perpetually out of my comfort zone.

—*Tory Burch*

It irritates me to be told how things always have been done. . . .

I defy the tyranny of precedent. I cannot afford the luxury of a closed mind.

—*Clara Barton*

Women must learn to find self-worth within themselves, not through others. It is important to carve out a place just for you.

—*Georgette Mosbacher*

→> • <←

Define success on your own terms, achieve it by your own rules, and build a life you're proud to live.

—*Anne Sweeney*

Don't be intimidated by what you don't know. That can be your greatest strength and ensure that you do things differently from everyone else.

—*Sara Blakely*

→→ • ←←

There is no female mind. The brain is not an organ of sex. Might as well speak of a female liver.

—*Charlotte Perkins Gilman*

The girls who were unanimously considered beautiful often rested on their beauty alone. I felt I had to do things.

—*Diane von Fürstenberg*

❋

What you do makes a difference, and you have to decide what kind of difference you want to make.

—*Jane Goodall*

I would have girls regard themselves not as adjectives, but as nouns.

—*Elizabeth Cady Stanton*

Your inability to
see yourself clearly
is what's keeping
you alive.

—*Sarah Silverman*

I'm no longer accepting the things I cannot change. I'm changing the things I cannot accept.

—*Angela Davis*

I always did something I was a little not ready to do. I think that's how you grow. When there's that moment of "Wow, I'm not really sure I can do this," and you push through those moments, that's when you have a breakthrough.

—*Marissa Mayer*

If you haven't forgiven yourself something, how can you forgive others?

—*Dolores Huerta*

Stand before the people you fear and speak your mind—even if your voice shakes.

—*Maggie Kuhn*

It is not easy to be a pioneer—but oh, it is fascinating! I would not trade one moment, even the worst moment, for all the riches in the world.

—*Elizabeth Blackwell*

Girls are not socialized to toot their own horns. But bosses aren't mind readers.

Speak up and let people know what you've done and what you want.

—*Irene Rosenfeld*

I have frequently been questioned, especially by women, of how I could reconcile family life with a scientific career. Well, it has not been easy.

—*Marie Curie*

❊

Trust your instincts. Lots of people will give you advice, and depending on how well they know you, the advice might be valid or not so valid. But at the end of the day, you know yourself best and you know what works best for you. . . . Don't doubt yourself.

—*Abigail Johnson*

If you don't risk
anything, you
risk even more.

—Erica Jong

# No one provokes me with impunity.

—*Mary, Queen of Scots*

Rather, ten times, die in the surf, heralding the way to a new world, than stand idly on the shore.

—*Florence Nightingale*

❋

My mother told me to be a lady. And for her, that meant be your own person, be independent.

—*Ruth Bader Ginsburg*

Make the most of yourself by fanning the tiny, inner sparks of possibility into flames of achievement.

—*Golda Meir*

➤➤ ● ◄◄

What's the greater risk? Letting go of what people think, or letting go of how I feel, what I believe, and who I am?

—*Brené Brown*

Wear your heart
on your skin
in this life.

—*Sylvia Plath*

One must be frank
to be relevant.

—*Corazon Aquino*

One does not always do the best there is. One does the best one can.

*—Catherine the Great*

There will not be a magic day when we wake up and it's now okay to express ourselves publicly. We make that day by doing things publicly until it's simply the way things are.

*—Tammy Baldwin*

Drama is very important in life: You have to come on with a bang.

# You never want to go out with a whimper.

—*Julia Child*

I can't be a rose

# in any man's lapel.

—Margaret Trudeau

You cannot divide creative juices from human juices. And as long as juicy women are equated with bad women, we will err on the side of being bad.

—*Erica Jong*

❈

A mistake is simply another way of doing things.

—*Katharine Graham*

I want to make sure we use all our talent, not just 25 percent.

—*Mae Jemison*

❀

I am glad that I paid so little attention to good advice; had I abided by it I might have been saved from some of my most valuable mistakes.

—*Edna St. Vincent Millay*

The right way is not always the popular and easy way. Standing for right when it is unpopular is a true test of moral character.

—*Margaret Chase Smith*

❀

I'm not worried. I'm in control.

—*Gloria Macapagal Arroyo*

There is a
special place in
hell for women
who do not help
other women.

—Madeleine K. Albright

In order to be
irreplaceable,
one must always
*be different.*

—*Coco Chanel*

I didn't get there by wishing for it or hoping for it,
but by working for it.

—*Estée Lauder*

❈

The difference between successful people and
others is how long they spend time feeling sorry for
themselves.

—*Barbara Corcoran*

Being human means throwing your whole life on the scales of destiny when need be, all the while rejoicing in every sunny day and every beautiful cloud.

—*Rosa Luxemburg*

⤞ • ⤝

Tremendous amounts of talent are lost to our society just because that talent wears a skirt.

—*Shirley Chisholm*

We teach girls to shrink themselves, to make themselves smaller. We say to girls, you can have ambition, but not too much. You should aim to be successful, but not too successful. Otherwise, you would threaten the man.

—*Chimamanda Ngozi Adichie*

Often we women are risk-averse. I needed the push. Now, more than ever, young women need more seasoned women to provide that encouragement, to take a risk, to go for it. Once a glass ceiling is broken, it stays broken.

—*Jennifer Granholm*

❅

I'm not fancy. I'm what I appear to be.

—*Janet Reno*

I learned to always take on things I'd never done before. Growth and comfort do not coexist.

—*Ginni Rometty*

In order to be irreplaceable, one must always be different.

—Coco Chanel

I've spent my whole life not talking to people, and I don't see why I should start now.

*—Sally Ride*

→> • <←

The only way to escape fear is to trample it beneath your feet.

*—Nadia Comăneci*

Above all, be the heroine of your life, not the victim.

—*Nora Ephron*

❊

I married beneath me—all women do.

—*Nancy Astor*

# Some leaders are *born women*.

—*Geraldine Ferraro*

Nasty women are tough. Nasty women are smart. And nasty women vote.

—*Elizabeth Warren*

The single best thing about honesty is that it requires no follow-up.

—*Rachel Maddow*

□

I have sometimes been wildly, despairingly, acutely miserable, racked with sorrow, but through it all I still know quite certainly that just to be alive is a grand thing.

—*Agatha Christie*

The sight of women talking together has always made men uneasy; nowadays it means rank subversion.

—*Germaine Greer*

❀

No one can make you feel inferior without your consent.

—*Eleanor Roosevelt*

A sex symbol becomes a thing. *I just hate to be a thing.* But if I'm going to be a symbol of something, I'd rather have it be sex than some other things they've got symbols of.

—*Marilyn Monroe*

Women have been called queens for a long time, but the kingdom given them isn't worth ruling.

—*Louisa May Alcott*

Whatever you want in life, other people are going to want it, too. Believe in yourself enough to accept the idea that you have an equal right to it.

—*Diane Sawyer*

❊

I love people. I love my family, my children . . . but inside myself is a place where I live all alone and that's where you renew your springs that never dry up.

—*Pearl Buck*

Well, knowledge is a fine thing, and mother Eve
thought so; but she smarted so severely for hers, that
most of her daughters have been afraid of it since.

—*Abigail Adams*

＋＞　•　＜＋

That would be a good thing for them to cut on my
tombstone: "Wherever she went, including here, it
was against her better judgment."

—*Dorothy Parker*

The connections between and among women are the most feared, the most problematic, and the most potentially transforming force on the planet.

—*Adrienne Rich*

➤ • ◂

Working hard becomes a habit, a serious kind of fun.

—*Mary Lou Retton*

And the day came when the risk to remain tight in a bud was more painful than the risk it took to blossom.

—*Anaïs Nin*

※

I've always been an angel. Sometimes I transform into a witch only because the filmmaking demands it.

—*Lina Wertmüller*

When men reach their sixties and retire, they go to pieces. WOMEN GO RIGHT ON COOKING.

—*Gail Sheehy*

Some people say I have attitude— maybe I do. But I think you have to. You have to believe

in yourself
when no one
else does.
That makes
you a winner
right there.

—*Venus Williams*

You can't please everyone and you can't make everyone like you.

—*Katie Couric*

✦

I totally and completely admit, with no qualms at all, my egomania, my selfishness, coupled with a really magnificent voice.

—*Leontyne Price*

It fills me with a weird rage to wear shoes that make me not able to walk easily or run if I had to. It feeds into this whole war on women thing in my head.

—*Sarah Silverman*

I still believe I'm the best player. That's what keeps me going.

—*Lisa Leslie*

So many women just don't know how great they really are. They come to us all vogue outside and vague on the inside.

—*Mary Kay Ash*

✳

Asking what I considered an impossible salary when I didn't want to work for someone has boosted my pay again and again.

—*Ethel Waters*

Nobody needs to prove to anybody what they're worthy of, just the person that they look at in the mirror.

—*Picabo Street*

❃

When someone tells you that you are different, smile and hold your head up and be proud.

—*Angelina Jolie*

I can never be safe;
I always try and go
against the grain. As
soon as I accomplish
one thing, *I just
set a higher goal.*

—*Beyoncé*

No matter how difficult and painful it may be, nothing sounds as good to the soul as the truth.

—Martha Beck

I think being a woman is like being Irish. Everyone says you're important and nice, but you take second place all the same.

—*Iris Murdoch*

➤➤ • ◄◄

There are some people who leave impressions not so lasting as the imprint of an oar upon the water.

—*Kate Chopin*

The thing that drives me most crazy in the world is not to be believed.

—*Nan Goldin*

❁

All issues are women's issues—and there are several that are just women's business.

—*Eddie Bernice Johnson*

I take care of my flowers and my cats. And enjoy food. And that's living.

—Ursula Andress

I just love bossy women. I could be around them all day. To me, bossy is not a pejorative term at all. It means somebody's passionate and engaged and ambitious and doesn't mind leading.

*—Amy Poehler*

I learned long ago that there is something worse than missing the goal, and that's not pulling the trigger.

*—Mia Hamm*

Instead of looking at the past, I put myself ahead twenty years and try to look at what I need to do now in order to get there then.

—*Diana Ross*

The minute you settle for less than you deserve, you get even less than you settled for.

—*Maureen Dowd*

What a wonderful
life I've had! I only
wish I'd realized
it sooner.

—*Colette*

People always call it luck when you've acted more sensibly than they have.

—*Anne Tyler*

❈

Nothing is ever the same as they said it was.

—*Diane Arbus*

Be passionate and move forward with gusto every single hour of every single day until you reach your goal.

—*Ava DuVernay*

It took me quite
a long time
to develop a
voice, and now
that I have it, I
am not going
to be silent.

—Madeleine K. Albright

Life is short. People are not easy to know. They're not easy to know, so if you don't tell them how you feel, you're not going to get anywhere.

—*Nina Simone*

❋

After all those years as a woman hearing "not thin enough, not pretty enough, not smart enough, not this enough, not that enough," almost overnight I woke up one morning and thought, "I'm enough."

—*Anna Quindlen*

You don't learn from successes; you don't learn from awards; you don't learn from celebrity; you only learn from wounds and scars and mistakes and failures. And that's the truth.

—*Jane Fonda*

# The truth will set you free, but first it will piss you off.

—Gloria Steinem

# Despite all the challenges we face, I remain convinced that yes, the future is female.

—Hillary Clinton

# SOURCES

Bella Abzug, 1920–1998, lawyer, U.S. representative, and leading feminist

Abigail Adams, 1744–1818, First Lady of the United States from 1797 to 1801

Chimamanda Ngozi Adichie, b. 1977, novelist

Madeleine K. Albright, b. 1937, first female U.S. Secretary of State

Louisa May Alcott, 1832–1888, novelist and poet

Sadie Tanner Mossell Alexander, 1898–1989, attorney

Isabel Allende, b. 1942, writer

Gloria Allred, b. 1941, civil rights attorney

Marian Anderson, 1897–1993, classical singer

Ursula Andress, b. 1936, actress

Maya Angelou, 1928–2014, poet and civil rights activist

Susan B. Anthony, 1820–1906, women's rights activist

Corazon Aquino, 1933–2009, first female president of the Philippines

Diane Arbus, 1923–1971, photographer

Elizabeth Arden, 1878–1966, businessperson

Gloria Macapagal Arroyo, b. 1947, president of the Philippines

Mary Kay Ash, 1918–2001, businessperson

Nancy Astor, 1879–1964, first female member of Parliament

Margaret Atwood, b. 1939, poet, novelist, and environmental activist

Jane Austen, 1775–1817, novelist

Iggy Azalea, b. 1990, rapper

Michelle Bachelet, b. 1951, president of Chile

Joan Baez, b. 1941, singer, songwriter, and activist

Pearl Bailey, 1918–1990, actress and singer

Ella Baker, 1903–1986, civil rights activist

Lucille Ball, 1911–1989, comedian, actress, and movie executive

Tallulah Bankhead, 1902–1968, actress

Josephine Baker, 1906–1975, singer and entertainer

Tammy Baldwin, b. 1962, U.S. senator

Brigitte Bardot, b. 1934, actress

Roseanne Barr, b. 1952, actress and comedian

Mary Barra, b. 1961, CEO and chair of General Motors

Gina Barreca, b. 1957, humorist and professor

Ethel Barrymore, 1879–1959, actress

Clara Barton, 1821–1912, nurse who founded the American Red Cross

Mary Catherine Bateson, b. 1929, anthropologist

Martha Beck, b. 1962, sociologist and author

Ingrid Bergman, 1915–1982, actress

Sandra Bernhard, b. 1955, comedian and actress

Sarah Bernhardt, 1844–1923, actress

Halle Berry, b. 1966, actress

Beyoncé, b. 1981, singer, songwriter, actress

Benazir Bhutto, 1953–2007, first female prime minister of Pakistan

Simone Biles, b. 1997, most decorated American gymnast and record-
holder of most gold medals in women's gymnastics at a single Games

Juliette Binoche, b. 1964, actress

Elizabeth Blackwell, 1821–1910, first woman in the United States
to earn a medical degree

Bonnie Blair, b. 1964, speed skater

Sara Blakely, b. 1971, founder of Spanx

Amelia Bloomer, 1818–1894, temperance and women's rights activist

Judy Blume, b. 1938, novelist

Nellie Bly, 1864–1922, journalist

Grace Lee Boggs, 1915–2015, social activist and philosopher

Boudicca, c. 30–61 AD, Celtic queen who led a revolt against Rome

Mika Brzezinski, b. 1967, television host and political commentator

Fanny Brice, 1891–1951, comedian, singer, and actress

Charlotte Brontë, 1816–1855, novelist and poet

Geraldine Brooks, b. 1955, journalist and novelist

Gwendolyn Brooks, 1917–2000, poet

Brené Brown, b. 1965, author and professor

Helen Gurley Brown, 1922–2012, author and publisher

Rita Mae Brown, b. 1944, writer and feminist

Pearl Buck, 1892–1973, novelist

Sandra Bullock, b. 1964, actress

Tory Burch, b. 1966, fashion designer

Barbara Bush, b. 1925, First Lady of the United States
    from 1989 to 1993

Candace Bushnell, b. 1958, novelist and television producer

Yancy Butler, b. 1970, actress

A. S. Byatt, b. 1936, novelist and poet

Susan Cain, b. 1968, writer and lecturer

Rosalynn Carter, b. 1927, First Lady of the United States
    from 1977 to 1981

Mary Cassatt, 1844–1926, painter

Willa Cather, 1873–1947, novelist

Catherine the Great, 1729–1796, longest-ruling female monarch
    of Russia

Carrie Chapman Catt, 1859–1947, founder of the League
    of Women Voters

Edith Cavell, 1865–1915, British nurse executed by Germans
    during WWI

Coco Chanel, 1883–1971, fashion designer

Cher, b. 1946, singer and actress

Judy Chicago, b. 1939, artist

Julia Child, 1912–2004, chef, author, and television personality

Lydia Maria Child, 1802–1880, abolitionist and women's rights activist

Shirley Chisholm, 1924–2005, first African American woman elected to U.S. Congress

Margaret Cho, b. 1968, comedian and actress

Pema Chödrön, b. 1936, Buddhist teacher

Kate Chopin, 1850–1904, novelist and short-story writer

Agatha Christie, 1890–1976, writer

Julie Christie, b. 1940, actress

Cleopatra, 69–30 BC, queen of Egypt

Chelsea Clinton, b. 1980, daughter of Bill and Hillary Clinton

Hillary Clinton, b. 1947, former First Lady, former Secretary of State, former Senator, and first female major-party candidate for president

Amal Clooney, b. 1978, lawyer and human rights activist

Bessie Coleman, 1892–1926, first African American to hold a pilot's license

Colette, 1873–1954, novelist

Nadia Comăneci, b. 1961, first gymnast in Olympic history to get a perfect score

Misty Copeland, b. 1982, ballet dancer

Barbara Corcoran, b. 1949, businessperson and columnist

Katie Couric, b. 1957, journalist and television anchor

Laverne Cox, b. 1984, transgender actress

Marie Curie, 1867–1934, physicist and chemist, first female Nobel Prize laureate and the only woman to be awarded twice, with the 1903 Nobel Prize in Physics and the 1911 Nobel Prize in Chemistry

Nicole Curtis, b. 1976, home-improvement television host

Mary Daly, 1928–2010, feminist and theologian

Angela Davis, b. 1944, radical political activist

Bette Davis, 1908–1989, actress

Dorothy Day, 1897–1980, journalist and social activist

Barbara De Angelis, b. 1951, television personality and writer

Simone de Beauvoir, 1908–1986, existentialist philosopher and writer

Ruby Dee, 1922–2014, actress and civil rights activist

Agnes de Mille, 1905–1993, dancer and choreographer

Zooey Deschanel, b. 1980, actress

Germaine de Staël, 1766–1817, writer and opponent of Napoleon

Gail Devers, b. 1966, U.S. Olympic champion in track

Princess Diana, 1961–1997, philanthropist; Princess of Wales; married to Charles, Prince of Wales, heir apparent of Queen Elizabeth II

Marlene Dietrich, 1901–1992, actress and singer

Emily Dickinson, 1830–1886, poet

Joan Didion, b. 1934, journalist and writer

Isak Dinesen (pseudonym of Karen Blixen), 1885–1962, author

Gabby Douglas, b. 1995, U.S. Olympic gymnast

Maureen Dowd, b. 1952, columnist and author

Isadora Duncan, 1877–1927, dancer

Ava DuVernay, b. 1972, director

Andrea Dworkin, 1946–2005, radical feminist

Amelia Earhart, 1897–1937, aviation pioneer

Marian Wright Edelman, b. 1939, founder of the Children's Defense Fund

Barbara Ehrenreich, b. 1941, author and political activist

George Eliot (pen name for Mary Anne Evans), 1819–1880, novelist and poet

Elizabeth I, 1533–1603, Queen of England

Elizabeth II, b. 1926, Queen of England

Gertrude B. Elion, 1918–1999, 1988 Nobel Prize laureate in Physiology or Medicine

Linda Ellerbee, b. 1944, journalist

Nora Ephron, 1941–2012, journalist, novelist, and screenwriter

Clarissa Pinkola Estés, b. 1945, poet and psychoanalyst

Susan Faludi, b. 1959, journalist

Vera Farmiga, b. 1973, actress

Farrah Fawcett, 1947–2009, actress

Dianne Feinstein, b. 1933, U.S. senator

Geraldine Ferraro, 1935–2011, U.S. representative, first major
    party candidate for vice president

Tina Fey, b. 1970, comedian, writer, and actress

Sally Field, b. 1946, actress

Vigdís Finnbogadóttir, b. 1930, president of Iceland

Carrie Fisher, 1956–2016, actress and writer

Jane Fonda, b. 1937, actress and political activist

Dame Margot Fonteyn, 1919–1991, ballet dancer

Betty Ford, 1918–2011, First Lady of the United States
    from 1974 to 1977

Jodie Foster, b. 1962, actress and filmmaker

Megan Fox, b. 1986, actress and model

Bethenny Frankel, b. 1970, reality television personality

Aretha Franklin, b. 1942, singer

Missy Franklin, b. 1995, Olympic gold medal winner in swimming

Zsa Zsa Gabor, 1917–2016, actress and socialite

Indira Gandhi, 1917–1984, Prime Minister of India

Judy Garland, 1922–1969, singer and actress

Melinda Gates, b. 1964, philanthropist

Roxane Gay, b. 1974, feminist writer

Leymah Gbowee, b. 1972, Nobel Peace Prize winner from Liberia

Althea Gibson, 1927–2003, first African American tennis champion

Gabrielle Giffords, b. 1970, former U.S. representative who survived
assassination attempt

Elizabeth Gilbert, b. 1969, author and memoirist

Charlotte Perkins Gilman, 1860–1935, author and feminist

Ruth Bader Ginsburg, b. 1933, U.S. Supreme Court Justice

Whoopi Goldberg, b. 1955, actress, comedian, and television host

Nan Goldin, b. 1953, photographer

Emma Goldman, 1869–1940, anarchist political activist

Maud Gonne, 1866–1953, Irish revolutionary

Jane Goodall, b. 1934, anthropologist and expert on chimpanzees

Ruth Gordon, 1896–1985, actress and screenwriter

Katharine Graham, 1917–2001, owner and publisher of
    *The Washington Post*

Martha Graham, 1894–1991, dancer and choreographer

Temple Grandin, b. 1947, autism spokesperson and professor
    of animal science

Jennifer Granholm, b. 1959, politician and attorney

Germaine Greer, b. 1939, writer and feminist leader

Angelina Grimké, 1805–1879, abolitionist and advocate for women's rights

Sarah Moore Grimké, 1792–1873, abolitionist and advocate
    for women's rights

Zaha Hadid, 1950–2016, architect

Fannie Lou Hamer, 1917–1977, civil rights activist

Bethany Hamilton, b. 1990, professional surfer and shark-attack
    survivor

Mia Hamm, b. 1972, former professional soccer player and
    Olympic gold medalist

Lorraine Hansberry, 1930–1965, first African American woman to write a play performed on Broadway

Mata Hari, 1876–1917, Dutch exotic dancer convicted of spying for Germany in WWI

Goldie Hawn, b. 1945, actress and producer

Carolyn Hax, b. 1966, advice columnist

Helen Hayes, 1900–1993, actress

Dorothy Irene Height, 1912–2010, civil rights and women's rights activist

Lillian Hellman, 1905–1984, playwright and screenwriter

Audrey Hepburn, 1929–1993, actress and humanitarian

Katharine Hepburn, 1907–2003, actress

Anita Hill, b. 1956, attorney and professor

Billie Holiday, 1915–1959, singer and songwriter

bell hooks, b. 1952, author and social activist

Marya Hornbacher, b. 1974, author

Lena Horne, 1917–2010, singer, dancer, and actress

Whitney Houston, 1963–2012, singer and actress

Julia Ward Howe, 1819–1910, wrote words to "The Battle Hymn of the Republic"

Vanessa Hudgens, b. 1988, singer and actress

Dolores Huerta, b. 1930, labor leader and civil rights activist

Zora Neale Hurston, 1891–1960, author

Molly Ivins, 1944–2007, columnist, journalist, and author

Glenda Jackson, b. 1936, actress and politician

Valerie Jarrett, b. 1956, lawyer and senior advisor to
    President Barack Obama

Marian Javits, 1925–2017, arts patron

Mae Jemison, b. 1956, first African American woman in space

Joan Jett, b. 1958, singer and songwriter

Joan of Arc, 1412–1431, martyr for France in the Hundred Years' War

Jewel, b. 1974, singer-songwriter

Abigail Johnson, b. 1961, president and CEO of Fidelity Investments

Eddie Bernice Johnson, b. 1935, U.S. representative

Lady Bird Johnson, 1912–2007, First Lady of the United States
    from 1963 to 1969

Sheila Johnson, b. 1949, businessperson and co-founder of BET; first
    African American woman to have a net worth of $1 billion

Angelina Jolie, b. 1975, actress, filmmaker, and humanitarian

Mother Jones (Mary Harris Jones), 1837–1930, labor organizer

Erica Jong, b. 1942, novelist and poet

Janis Joplin, 1943–1970, singer

Elena Kagan, b. 1960, U.S. Supreme Court Justice

Frida Kahlo, 1907–1954, artist

Helen Keller, 1880–1968, author and political activist, first deaf
and blind person to earn a bachelor's degree

Anna Kendrick, b. 1985, actress and singer

Jackie Kennedy, 1929–1994, First Lady of the United States
from 1961 to 1963

Billie Jean King, b. 1943, former professional tennis player

Carole King, b. 1942, singer, songwriter, and composer

Coretta Scott King, 1927–2006, civil rights leader and widow of Dr.
Martin Luther King, Jr.

Eartha Kitt, 1927–2008, singer, actress, and activist

Elisabeth Kübler-Ross, 1926–2004, psychiatrist

Maggie Kuhn, 1905–1995, founder of the Gray Panthers

Aung San Suu Kyi, b. 1945, Burmese politician under house arrest
for fifteen years

Winona LaDuke, b. 1959, environmentalist and writer, Green Party
candidate for vice president

Lady Gaga, b. 1986, singer, actress, and songwriter

Anne Lamott, b. 1954, writer

Ann Landers (pen name for Eppie Lederer), 1918–2002,
advice columnist

Dorothea Lange, 1895–1965, photographer

Queen Latifah, b. 1970, singer, songwriter, and television
producer and host

Estée Lauder, 1908–2004, businessperson

Fran Lebowitz, b. 1950, author

Harper Lee, 1926–2016, novelist

Ursula K. Le Guin, b. 1929, novelist

Annie Leibovitz, b. 1949, photographer

Lisa Leslie, b. 1972, professional women's basketball player

Doris Lessing, 1919–2013, essayist and novelist

Rita Levi-Montalcini, 1909–2012, 1986 Nobel Prize laureate in
Physiology or Medicine

Lili'uokalani, 1838–1917, last reigning monarch of the Kingdom
of Hawaii

Maya Lin, b. 1959, designer and artist

Anne Morrow Lindbergh, 1906–2001, author and aviator

Carli Lloyd, b. 1982, soccer player

Anita Loos, 1889–1981, screenwriter and author

Jennifer Lopez, b. 1969, singer, actress, and producer

Nancy Lopez, b. 1957, professional golfer

Audre Lorde, 1934–1992, writer and civil rights activist

Demi Lovato, b. 1992, singer and actress

Ada Lovelace, 1815–1852, mathematician and writer

Juliette Gordon Low, 1860–1927, founder of Girl Scouts of the USA

Clare Boothe Luce, 1903–1987, author, politician, and
    U.S. ambassador to Brazil

Ida Lupino, 1918–1995, actress, singer, director, and producer

Rosa Luxemburg, 1871–1919, revolutionary and philosopher

Mary Lyon, 1797–1849, leader in women's education

Beryl Markham, 1902–1986, first woman to fly solo across the Atlantic
    Ocean from east to west

Claire McCaskill, b. 1953, U.S. senator

LisaRaye McCoy, b. 1966, actress and designer

Hattie McDaniel, 1895–1952, actress and first African American
    to win an Academy Award

Reba McEntire, b. 1955, singer, songwriter, and actress

Shirley MacLaine, b. 1934, actress, singer, and author

Rachel Maddow, b. 1973, television host and political commentator

Madonna, b. 1958, singer and songwriter

Wilma Mankiller, 1945–2010, first female chief of the Cherokee Nation

Mary, Queen of Scots, 1542–1587, queen of Scotland

Marissa Mayer, b. 1975, CEO of Yahoo!

Margaret Mead, 1901–1978, anthropologist

Golda Meir, 1898–1978, Prime Minister of Israel

Angela Merkel, b. 1954, chancellor of Germany

Joyce Meyer, b. 1943, Christian author and speaker

Bette Midler, b. 1945, singer, actress, and producer

Barbara Mikulski, b. 1936, U.S. senator and U.S. representative

Edna St. Vincent Millay, 1892–1950, poet and playwright

Kate Millett, b. 1934, feminist writer and activist

Nicki Minaj, b. 1982, rapper, singer, and songwriter

Helen Mirren, b. 1945, actress

Janelle Monáe, b. 1985, singer and actress

Marilyn Monroe, 1926–1962, actress

Marianne Moore, 1887–1972, poet

Mary Tyler Moore, 1936–2017, actress

Hannah More, 1745–1833, writer and philanthropist

Jeanne Moreau, b. 1928, actress and director

Robin Morgan, b. 1941, feminist writer and activist

Toni Morrison, b. 1931, novelist

Georgette Mosbacher, b. 1947, business entrepreneur and
    political activist

Kate Moss, b. 1974, model

Iris Murdoch, 1919–1999, novelist

Emily Murphy, 1868–1933, women's rights activist

Caroline Myss, b. 1952, author

Martina Navratilova, b. 1956, twenty-time Wimbledon tennis winner

Anna Netrebko, b. 1971, opera singer

Louise Nevelson, 1899–1988, sculptor

Caroline Nichols Churchill, 1833–1926, writer

Florence Nightingale, 1820–1910, nurse and nurse trainer

Anaïs Nin, 1903–1977, writer

Peggy Noonan, b. 1950, author, columnist, and presidential speechwriter

Diana Nyad, b. 1949, long-distance swimmer

Annie Oakley, 1860–1926, Western performer

Michelle Obama, b. 1964, attorney and First Lady of the United States
from 2009 to 2017

Flannery O'Connor, 1925–1964, writer and essayist

Georgia O'Keeffe, 1887–1986, artist

Yoko Ono, b. 1933, artist, singer, and peace activist

Marie Osmond, b. 1959, singer and actress

Camille Paglia, b. 1947, social critic

Christabel Pankhurst, 1880–1958, women's suffrage activist

Emmeline Pankhurst, 1858–1928, leader of British women's
suffrage movement

Dorothy Parker, 1893–1967, short-story writer and critic

Sarah Jessica Parker, b. 1965, actress and producer

Rosa Parks, 1913–2005, civil rights activist

Danica Patrick, b. 1982, stock car racer

Alice Paul, 1885–1977, women's rights activist

Jane Pauley, b. 1950, journalist and author

Nancy Pelosi, b. 1940, minority leader of the U.S. House of Representatives

Frances Perkins, 1880–1965, workers' rights advocate and U.S. Secretary of Labor

Marge Piercy, b. 1936, poet and novelist

Pink, b. 1979, singer and songwriter

Sylvia Plath, 1932–1963, poet

Amy Poehler, b. 1971, actress, comedian, and writer

Natalie Portman, b. 1981, actress

Leontyne Price, b. 1927, classical singer

Annie Proulx, b. 1935, novelist

Anna Quindlen, b. 1952, journalist and writer

Gilda Radner, 1946–1989, comedian

Rania of Jordan, b. 1970, queen consort of Jordan

Ayn Rand, 1905–1982, novelist and philosopher

Phylicia Rashad, b. 1948, actress, singer, and director

Maureen Reagan, 1941–2001, daughter of President Ronald Reagan

Nancy Reagan, 1921–2016, actress and First Lady of the United States from 1981 to 1989

Ruth Reichl, b. 1948, chef and food writer

Kathy Reichs, b. 1948, forensic anthropologist and crime writer

Janet Reno, 1938–2016, first female U.S. attorney general

Mary Lou Retton, b. 1968, Olympic gold medal–winning gymnast

Shonda Rhimes, b. 1970, television producer and author

Condoleezza Rice, b. 1954, U.S. Secretary of State and political scientist

Adrienne Rich, 1929–2012, poet

Ann Richards, 1933–2006, governor of Texas

Sally Ride, 1951–2012, first American woman in space

Rihanna, b. 1988, singer and songwriter

Joan Rivers, 1933–2014, comedian and writer

Julia Roberts, b. 1967, actress

Mary Robinson, b. 1944, first female president of Ireland

Ginger Rogers, 1911–1995, dancer and actress

Ginni Rometty, b. 1957, first woman to head IBM as chair, president, and CEO

Eleanor Roosevelt, 1884–1962, longest-serving First Lady of the United States (1933–1945), diplomat, and activist

Irene Rosenfeld, b. 1953, business executive

Diana Ross, b. 1944, singer, songwriter, and actress

Ronda Rousey, b. 1987, mixed martial artist and actress

Dilma Rousseff, b. 1947, president of Brazil

J. K. Rowling, b. 1965, novelist and screenwriter

Helena Rubinstein, 1872–1965, cosmetics entrepreneur

Wilma Rudolph, 1940–1994, Olympic track champion

Rosalind Russell, 1907–1976, actress

Sacagawea, 1788–1812, female member of Shoshone tribe who helped guide the Lewis and Clark expedition

George Sand, 1804–1876, novelist and memoirist

Sheryl Sandberg, b. 1969, chief operating officer of Facebook and author

Margaret Sanger, 1879–1966, opened first birth control clinic in the United States

Sappho, 620–550 BC, Greek poet

Diane Sawyer, b. 1945, television journalist

Patricia Schroeder, b. 1940, U.S. representative

Amy Schumer, b. 1981, comedian, writer, and actress

Hazel Scott, 1920–1981, pianist and singer

Amy Sedaris, b. 1961, author, comedian, and actress

Carolyn See, 1934–2016, author

Shakira, b. 1977, singer, dancer, and songwriter

Anna Howard Shaw, 1847–1919, physician and leader of women's suffrage movement

Gail Sheehy, b. 1937, journalist and author

Mary Shelley, 1797–1851, novelist

Carol Shields, 1935–2003, novelist

Sarah Silverman, b. 1970, comedian and writer

Carly Simon, b. 1945, singer-songwriter

Nina Simone, 1933–2003, singer, songwriter, and civil rights activist

Ellen Johnson Sirleaf, b. 1938, president of Liberia

Cornelia Otis Skinner, 1899–1979, actress and writer

B. Smith, b. 1949, model, author, and restaurateur

Margaret Chase Smith, 1897–1995, first woman to serve
in both houses of Congress

Patti Smith, b. 1946, singer and poet

Zadie Smith, b. 1975, novelist

Olympia Snowe, b. 1947, U.S. senator

Susan Sontag, 1933–2004, writer and political activist

Sonia Sotomayor, b. 1954, U.S. Supreme Court Justice

Muriel Spark, 1918–2006, novelist, poet, and essayist

Elizabeth Cady Stanton, 1815–1902, abolitionist and women's
movement leader

Gertrude Stein, 1874–1946, novelist and poet

Gloria Steinem, b. 1934, journalist and feminist leader

Martha Stewart, b. 1941, writer, businessperson, and television
personality

Meryl Streep, b. 1949, actress

Picabo Street, b. 1971, Olympic gold medalist in alpine ski racing

Pat Summitt, 1952–2016, winningest women's college basketball coach in history

Anne Sweeney, b. 1957, former co-chair of Disney Media

Ida M. Tarbell, 1857–1944, journalist

Elizabeth Taylor, 1932–2011, actress

Sara Teasdale, 1884–1933, poet

Margaret Thatcher, 1925–2013, first female British prime minister

Helen Thomas, 1920–2013, journalist

Lily Tomlin, b. 1939, comedian, actress, and writer

Margaret Trudeau, b. 1948, author and actress, married to Canadian Prime Minister Pierre Trudeau and mother of Canadian Prime Minister Justin Trudeau

Sojourner Truth, 1797–1883, abolitionist and women's rights activist

Harriet Tubman, 1820–1913, former slave, rescued slaves through Underground Railroad

Robin Tunney, b. 1972, actress

Tina Turner, b. 1939, singer, dancer, and actress

Anne Tyler, b. 1941, novelist

Cicely Tyson, b. 1924, actress

Laurel Thatcher Ulrich, b. 1938, historian

Abigail Van Buren (pen name for Pauline Phillips), 1918–2013, advice
columnist

Queen Victoria, 1819–1901, Queen of United Kingdom

Diane von Fürstenberg, b. 1946, fashion designer

Alice Walker, b. 1944, novelist, poet, and activist

Madame C. J. Walker, 1867–1919, business entrepreneur and
civil rights activist

Barbara Walters, b. 1929, broadcast journalist

Abby Wambach, b. 1980, Olympic gold medalist in soccer

Elizabeth Warren, b. 1949, academic and U.S. Senator

Kerry Washington, b. 1977, actress

Martha Washington, 1731–1802, first First Lady of the
United States (1789–1797)

Wendy Wasserstein, 1950–2006, playwright

Ethel Waters, 1896–1977, singer and actress

Maxine Waters, b. 1938, U.S. representative

Emma Watson, b. 1990, actress

Faye Wattleton, b. 1943, feminist activist, former president
of Planned Parenthood

Raquel Welch, b. 1940, actress

Ida B. Wells, 1862–1931, journalist and feminist

Lina Wertmüller, b. 1928, screenwriter and film director

Mae West, 1893–1980, actress

Rebecca West, 1892–1983, journalist and writer

Edith Wharton, 1862–1937, author

Betty White, b. 1922, actress

Kristen Wiig, b. 1973, actress, comedian, and writer

Samira Wiley, b. 1987, actress

Serena Williams, b. 1981, professional tennis player

Venus Williams, b. 1980, professional tennis player

Marianne Williamson, b. 1952, author and lecturer

Amy Winehouse, 1983–2011, singer and songwriter

Oprah Winfrey, b. 1954, media entrepreneur, former talk show host, and philanthropist

Shelley Winters, 1920–2006, actress

Naomi Wolf, b. 1962, author and political advisor

Victoria Woodhull, 1838–1927, publisher and women's rights activist

Virginia Woolf, 1882–1941, writer

Kristi Yamaguchi, b. 1971, champion figure skater

Janet Yellen, b. 1946, economist and chair of the Board of Governors of the Federal Reserve System

Loretta Young, 1913–2000, actress

Malala Yousafzai, b. 1997, Pakistani activist for education of girls and women and youngest-ever Nobel Prize laureate for 2014 Nobel Peace Prize

Babe Didrikson Zaharias, 1911–1956, Olympic gold and silver medalist in track and field

Linda Picone is an editor and writer who has worked for newspapers and magazines and has written or edited a number of books, from *Caring for You and Your Baby* to *Carpe Diem*. She lives in Minneapolis and is proud to be known as a Nasty Woman on occasion.